St. Helena Library

D1505002

The history of emigration from
IRELAND

Katherine Prior

FRANKLIN WATTS
A Division of Grolier Publishing
NEW YORK • LONDON • HONG KONG • SYDNEY
DANBURY, CONNECTICUT

Copyright © Franklin Watts 1996
First American Edition 1997
by Franklin Watts
A Division of Grolier Publishing
Sherman Turnpike
Danbury, Connecticut 06816

Library of Congress Cataloging-in-Publication Data
Prior, Katherine.
     Ireland / Katherine Prior. — 1st
     American ed.
          p. cm. — (Origins)
     Includes bibliographical references (p.)
     and index.
     Summary: Discusses the history of
     Ireland, focusing on the various reasons
     for the large number of emigrants that
     left the country particularly beginning in
     the nineteenth century.
     ISBN 0-531-14415-1
     1. Ireland—History—Juvenile literature.
     [1. Ireland—History. 2. Ireland—
     Emigration and immigration.] 1. Title. II.
     Series: Origins (New York, N.Y.)
     DA911.P75 1997   96-4271
     941.5—dc20   CIP AC

Series editor: Rachel Cooke
Designer: Simon Borrough
Picture research: Brooks Krikler Research

Printed in Malaysia

Picture acknowledgements

t=top; b=bottom; m=middle; r=right; l=left
Kelvin Boyes p. 28t
Bridgeman Art Library pp. 7b, 8-9
James Davis Travel Photography p. 4
Department of Irish Folklore, University of Dublin
pp. 13, 17t
Leslie Dowley/Oak Park Research Centre p. 16r
Mary Evans Picture Library pp. 5b, 8, 9, 11br, 18tl
Eye Ubiquitous p. 6r
Robert Harding Picture Library pp. 5t, 10b
Hulton Deutsch Collection pp. 6bl, 7t, 10(t and m),
11bl, 12b, 21b, 23(ml and mr), 26t
Illustrated London News Picture Library pp. 14b,
16l, 17b, 18-19b, 19t, 25m
The Mansell Collection p. 12t
Museum of the City of New York pp. 23b, 24(both)
National Library of Ireland p. 19m
Range/Bettmann pp. 15, 20, 21t, 22(tr and b),
27(both) and 29(both)
Spectrum Colour Library pp. 14t, 25, 28b
Frank Spooner Pictures pp. 21tr, 22tl

Contents

Ireland: A Place to Leave?

A hundred years ago, in the 1890s, over a third of all the people born in Ireland no longer lived there.

ULSTER

Belfast

CONNAUGHT

Dublin

LEINSTER

MUNSTER

Cork

- - - NORTHERN IRELAND

Ireland is divided into four provinces. The poorest farmland is found in Connaught and Munster.

In the past 200 years, millions of Irish people have left their homes in Ireland and emigrated overseas. Most of this emigration occurred in the 19th century. A hundred years ago, in the 1890s, over a third of all the people born in Ireland no longer lived there; they had emigrated to England, Scotland, Australia, New Zealand, South Africa, Canada, and above all, the United States. Why did so many people uproot themselves, leaving behind their homes and friends? To answer this question we need first to know something about the living conditions in Ireland at the beginning of the 19th century.

A wet, green land

Ireland is a wet country, lushly carpeted in grass. The grass is excellent for raising sheep and cattle, but the high rainfall makes it difficult to grow cereal crops such as wheat, barley, and oats. Whereas in other countries poor people often lived on bread and other foodstuffs made from cereals, in Ireland grain was too expensive for most people to eat. Instead they lived on potatoes, which were easy to grow and did not take up much land.

In 1800 Ireland had a population of about 5 million which was increasing rapidly. A few wealthy landlords owned nearly all of the land. They let out their land to tenant farmers, some of whom were prosperous and had good-sized farms. Three-quarters of the population, however, were poor peasants – some were able to rent scraps of farming land, but this left them with almost no extra money. Many were too poor to rent land. Instead they worked as day laborers, traveling from farm to farm looking for odd jobs.

The laborers and small farmers lived simply in cottages with mud floors and low, thatched roofs. Most farmers and their families did not eat any grain that they grew but sold it for cash and lived on potatoes instead.

A farming life

In the 19th century, farming was almost the only source of work in Ireland, and as the population increased, unemployment became a serious problem. In England and Scotland, the Industrial Revolution was taking place, and from all over the countryside people were shifting to cities such as London, Manchester, and Glasgow to work in new factories. Ireland, however, had almost no factory work and remained dependent on agricultural exports. Instead of building their own factories, merchants in Ireland found that they could make money more quickly by selling Ireland's raw products, such as flax (for making linen) and wool, direct to factories in Britain.

▲ Wealthy landlords lived in grand houses known simply as "big houses," such as this one in County Sligo.

▼ By contrast, a laborer's cottage was small and dark. Living conditions were extremely cramped.

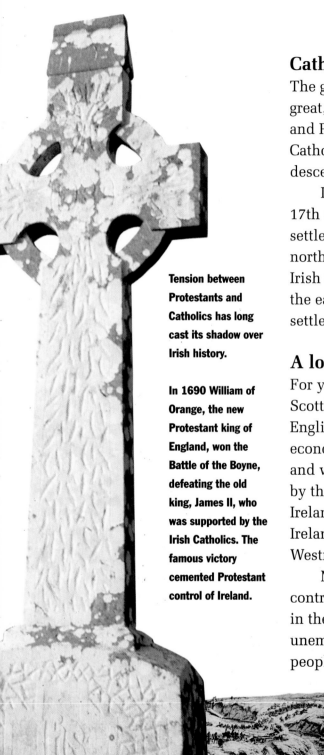

Tension between Protestants and Catholics has long cast its shadow over Irish history.

In 1690 William of Orange, the new Protestant king of England, won the Battle of the Boyne, defeating the old king, James II, who was supported by the Irish Catholics. The famous victory cemented Protestant control of Ireland.

Catholics versus Protestants

The gap between landlords and peasants in Ireland was great, but Irish society was also divided between Catholics and Protestants. Most native Irish, who spoke Gaelic, were Catholics. The Protestants, who spoke English, were the descendants of old settlers from England and Scotland.

Ireland was a Catholic country, but in the 16th and 17th centuries English and Scottish Protestants began to settle in Ireland, especially on the rich farmland of the northern province of Ulster. They pushed out the native Irish Catholic farmers onto poor, unproductive lands. By the early 19th century the descendants of these Protestant settlers made up about 20 percent of Ireland's population.

A losing battle

For years the Irish fought back against the English and Scottish settlers, but they were repeatedly defeated by the English armies and Catholics were slowly deprived of their economic and political power. Soon nearly all the land and wealth in Ireland was owned by Protestants. In 1801, by the Act of Union, the Protestants agreed to abolish Ireland's parliament in Dublin. From 1801 until 1921, Ireland was ruled directly by the British parliament at Westminster in London.

Many Irish Catholics resented the British Protestant control of Ireland; they felt that they had become outsiders in their own country. This feeling, along with unemployment, poverty, and scarcity of land, made many people decide to emigrate from 19th century Ireland.

Sentenced to Exile

12-year-old James Blake from Dublin had been transported for stealing a silver spoon.

▲ Convicts awaiting transportation to Australia were held on prison ships anchored at ports in Britain and Ireland. These ships were old, unseaworthy hulks like the one above. The convicts were taken ashore every day to work in chain gangs and returned to the ships at night.

Most of Ireland's emigrants chose to leave their country, even if some did so reluctantly. One group of emigrants, however, had no choice at all. These were the convicts who were transported to the prison colony of Australia. Between 1788 and 1868, over 50,000 Irish men, women, and children were sent to Australia as prisoners. After their release most of them settled in Australia.

In 18th-century Britain and Ireland, minor crimes were punished harshly and someone caught stealing a sheep or shirt could be sentenced to many years in jail. The jails were soon overflowing and in the 1780s the government decided to ship some of its prison population to the far-off continent of Australia. The First Fleet of convict ships arrived off the east coast of Australia in January 1788 and a new British penal colony was established at Sydney Cove.

The first Irish transport

There were some Irish-born prisoners in the First Fleet, but *The Queen* was the first convict ship to sail directly from Ireland. She left Cork in April 1791 with a total of 133 male and 22 female prisoners onboard, including 12-year-old James Blake from Dublin who had stolen a silver spoon. Also onboard was Bridget McDonnel, aged 23, transported for stealing 11 yards of cotton cloth. A single mother, she took her year-old daughter, Betty, with her.

The Queen took almost six months to reach Sydney, by which time the convicts were nearly dead from starvation. A shocked naval officer described them as *"skeletons, apparently with a human skin drawn over the bones."* The captain of *The Queen* had underfed the convicts in order to sell the uneaten food at a profit in the new colony. Disease had also flourished in the crowded conditions on the ship, and seven convicts had died at sea.

▲ This picture of Sydney Cove dates from the early 1800s. The first convicts to arrive there found no houses or roads; they had to build everything from scratch.

A strange new land

On arrival in Australia everything seemed strange. The local people, the Aborigines, did not wear clothes or live in houses like Europeans. The climate was hot and dry and the trees were spindly. The animals seemed to belong to another world. The convicts from *The Queen* knew so little about their new home that in November 1791, just a month after arriving, 21 of them fled into the bush hoping to be able to walk to China. Two were killed by Aborigines and the remainder, exhausted and hungry and confused, were forced back to the convict settlement by the harsh climate and thick, impenetrable bush.

Work and punishment

Life for all the convicts in Australia was hard. The men were set to work clearing land, cutting stone, and building roads and houses. Often, because there was a shortage of horses, they did the work of animals and were chained together into plow or haulage gangs, driven by an overseer flourishing a whip. Punishments were severe: flogging, chain gangs, and solitary confinement were all used to break the spirit of rebellious convicts.

Women convicts were sent to work in prison factories, often making coarse clothes and sacking. Like the men,

European settlers in Australia had little respect for the "strange" Aborigines. They ruthlessly drove them off any land they wanted and many were killed.▼

▲ Women convicts who married a released convict or a settler were often granted their freedom.

they were punished for insolence and refusal to work, commonly by being fitted with a ball and chain or having their heads shaved.

Peasants and political prisoners

Many of the convicts sent directly from Ireland had little experience of life outside of their village. Once in Australia, these convicts stood out from the rest. Unlike the Scots and English convicts, they were mostly peasants, with no knowledge of city life. They were also usually Catholics, whereas most other convicts were Protestants.

One group of Irish convicts was different. These were the men exiled to Australia for leading rebellions in 1798 and 1848 against British rule in Ireland. They were few in number and they had little in common with the ordinary Irish convicts. But the convict guards became convinced that all the Irish convicts were political rebels and often singled them out for punishment. In 1800, for example, some convicts who were overheard speaking Gaelic were brought to trial for using a "secret language" to plan revolt. The Irish soon learned that it was safer to speak English and to blend in with the other convicts. As a result, they lost much of their traditional culture. In particular, knowledge of Gaelic died out quickly in Australia.

▲ This convict of the 1790s wore his own clothes. Later on, convicts had to wear uniforms.

Freedom

In spite of the harsh conditions, many Irish convicts eventually prospered in Australia. Convict sentences were reduced for good behavior and it was possible after four or five years in the colony to begin working for oneself. To encourage farming, the British government gave grants of land to freed convicts and in some cases agreed to send to Australia the wives and children of male convicts.

Convicts writing home to their families in Ireland often spoke happily of the opportunities they had gained in Australia where laborers were well paid. In 1840, a newly arrived convict, James Halloran, wrote to his wife telling her that Australia *"is the best country under the sun . . . "*

Another convict, William Moore, told his wife that even if he were free *"I would not go home for three or four years . . . . I am in a factuary making soap and candles since I came to the Country and as happy as I please."* Alexander Boyce, a convict from Belfast, wrote that *"there is no part of the world where an industrious man can do better."*

Transportation to Australia did not end until 1868, but by the 1830s and 1840s, the letters sent home to Ireland by convicts were encouraging their friends and neighbors to think of Australia not as a prison but as a land of promise.

The first farms in Australia were simple homesteads. Their owners had to work hard. But it was still a dream come true for many former Irish convicts.

Early drawings of kangaroos were often inaccurate.

The modern city of Sydney today is a tribute to the labor and suffering of the convicts who began building it over 200 years ago.

10

No Work, No Prospects

In the early 19th century, unemployment soared in Ireland. After 1815 and the end of the Napoleonic wars, prices for Ireland's grain exports slumped and, in an attempt to earn more money, many farmers switched from growing grain to breeding beef and dairy cattle, reducing the work available for farm laborers. As cheap yarns and cloths made in modern factories in Britain flooded the Irish market, many Irish weavers and spinners were thrown out of work. In 1829, one group of desperate cotton weavers from Cork begged the government to help them emigrate:

"We are in the most deplorable state of distress actually famishing for the want of employment . . . all our [clothes] are in pawn, [blankets] we have scarcely any . . . and expect daily to be turned out on the street. . . . We see no prospect but in emigration."

Harvesters and fishermen

Each spring thousands of Irish workers went to England and Scotland in search of summertime work. Some traveled to Kent in southeast England to pick hops for beermaking; others worked in the market gardens around London. Other seasonal workers went further abroad.

"The times are looking very hard,
The wages they are small.
So now I'm off to America,
Where there's work and food for all."

Seasonal labor could involve the whole family; in the hop-fields older children often looked after the younger ones while their parents worked. ◄

Seasonal labor kept people on the move. The workers got to see and hear about different parts of the world as they moved from one job to another. ▼

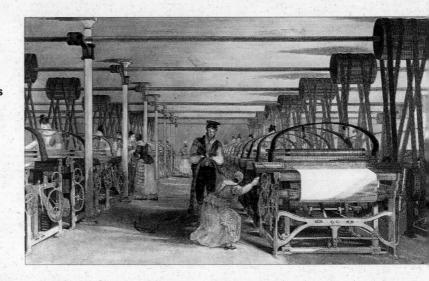

Many Irish emigrants found jobs in the textile factories of Lancashire in northwest England. Children were often hired to work in these factories because they were cheap, but it was dangerous work and many were killed or maimed by the weaving machinery.

Several thousand men from southeast Ireland used to sail across the Atlantic each spring to work in the fisheries of Newfoundland, returning to Ireland in the autumn with money saved up to boost the family budget.

The returning laborers brought news of the outside world to their families and neighbors. People who had never left their village in Ireland thus got to hear that good wages, cheap food, and year-round employment were available in Britain and North America. For some this was sufficient encouragement to pack up and leave Ireland.

Permanent migration across the Irish Sea

A trickle of Irish people had been emigrating to England and Scotland for centuries, but now thousands began to leave. By 1841, over 400,000 Irish people were living in British towns and cities.

In moving to Britain many emigrants found their lives turned upside down. Most of them were farm workers from the countryside. In Britain they had to adjust to life in bustling cities. Instead of agricultural labor they were now hired to work in factories or on construction sites. Women and children often became street vendors, selling cheap things like oranges, hair combs, or matches. Some of the women were engaged as domestic servants. Overall the Irish in 19th century Britain formed a reservoir of unskilled, cheap labor. They were often resented by English and Scottish workers because of their willingness to work for low wages.

Most Irish emigrants to Britain earned low wages. They could not afford good housing and were often crowded together in dark, unhealthy slums.

▲ The Irish immigrants to Britain settled in industrial cities, such as London, Glasgow, and Manchester, where factory and laboring work could be found. Their destination depended partly on the port they sailed from.

▼ Early Irish emigrants to North America were often prosperous, like the well-dressed family shown here, as they could finance the journey. A ticket to America often cost as much as a poor laborer would earn in a whole year.

When they left Ireland most emigrants had some idea of where they were going in Britain. They already had friends or relatives settled in Britain who helped them find housing and work. Where they went often determined what sort of work the emigrants did. For example, in Dundee the Irish found work in the linen mills; in Paisley and Greenock they worked in sugar refineries. Strong Irish communities gradually built up within particular towns and cities in Britain, who saw it as their duty to extend hospitality and help to any newcomers.

Links across the Atlantic

The Irish had a long tradition of emigrating to North America, but a ticket to cross the Atlantic was not cheap. In the 1830s it cost much more to sail to North America than it did to sail to London. In the first half of the 19th century, therefore, poor emigrants usually took the short, cheap journey to Scotland and England, whereas those better off went to North America. Protestant farmers from Ulster were prominent in this migration. They left Ireland not to avoid poverty but because they saw no hope of buying their own land or of improving their farms there.

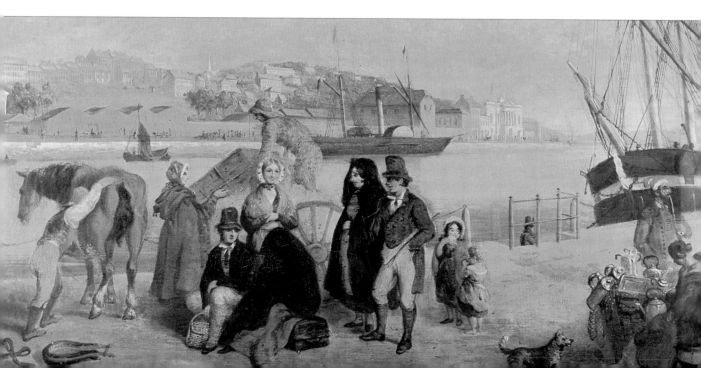

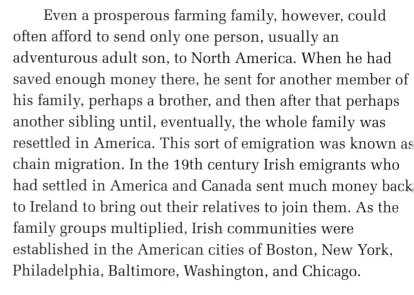

▲ Good quality farmland in Canada and the United States was cheap; many hard-pressed tenant farmers in Ireland were prepared to risk everything in the hope of buying a farm of their own in North America.

Weary emigrants found an alternative use for their trunks on the long journey across the Atlantic.▼

Even a prosperous farming family, however, could often afford to send only one person, usually an adventurous adult son, to North America. When he had saved enough money there, he sent for another member of his family, perhaps a brother, and then after that perhaps another sibling until, eventually, the whole family was resettled in America. This sort of emigration was known as chain migration. In the 19th century Irish emigrants who had settled in America and Canada sent much money back to Ireland to bring out their relatives to join them. As the family groups multiplied, Irish communities were established in the American cities of Boston, New York, Philadelphia, Baltimore, Washington, and Chicago.

Incentives to emigrate

It was a huge decision to emigrate to America; almost certainly it meant leaving Ireland forever. Often it was the letters that emigrants wrote back home that persuaded others to emigrate. Some letters told of hardship, and homesickness, but there were many more that painted a picture of America as a land of plenty, where work and land were bountiful. One tenant farmer who had emigrated to New York state and earned enough to buy a farm, wrote back home declaring with pride: *"No one can demand rent of me. My family and I eat our fill of bread and meat, butter and milk any day we like throughout the year."*

Another emigrant, a weaver, who arrived in America with only a few coins in his pocket, wrote to his family three years later with the news that he had purchased a house and land worth $200. Everyone in the village, he promised, could make a fortune if they came to America.

The rosy picture of America conveyed in emigrants' letters often found its way into folk songs like this one:

"The times are looking very hard,
The wages they are small.
So now I'm off to America,
Where there's work and food for all."

Other sources of information also encouraged people to emigrate. American construction companies advertised

in Irish newspapers for laborers to work on American roads and canals. Emigration agents, who made their living by arranging emigrants' voyages, put up all over Ireland posters advertising emigration. Land companies, with charters from the British government to open up farming land in the colonies of Canada and Australia,

also advertised for emigrants. In 1835 the British American Land Company advertised in the *Belfast Newsletter*: *"One Million Acres of Land, in Farms of 100 Acres and upwards, situated in the healthy and fertile Eastern Townships of Lower Canada."* For many struggling tenant farmers in Ireland the promise of cheap, fertile land in North America was too good to resist.

These cartoons represent the dreams and hopes of many Irish emigrants. On the left, a poor laborer thinks about emigrating to New York. The right-hand cartoon shows him after he has emigrated and has become a successful businessman. Now he is contemplating a trip back home to Ireland. In reality, however, most Irish men and women never returned to Ireland once they had left.

The Great Famine, 1845-1849

They ate wild grasses, nettles and leaves from trees in an attempt to keep alive.

During the famine, people of all ages died. Children were often orphaned and left to fend for themselves, like these children searching for unspoiled potatoes.

In the autumn of 1845 the potato harvest in Ireland was largely destroyed by a new disease. Potato blight, a type of fungus, turned the potates into a foul-smelling, black spongy mass (see the picture below). The harvest was ruined for four years in a row; not until 1850 was there a reliable potato crop again, by which time millions of Irish people had either died of starvation or emigrated.

When the potato crop failed, the British government was reluctant to implement relief measures on the massive scale needed to prevent widespread starvation. The government did import supplies of corn and set up public relief works for laborers, but these measures were hampered by inefficient organization and mean-spirited bureaucracy. Generally, the British authorities felt hand-outs to the starving peasants would encourage laziness.

Eviction and starvation

Unable to pay their rent, many starving tenant farmers and their families were evicted from their land. Others abandoned their homes in desperation and took to the roads, looking for any form of work or food. They ate wild grasses, nettles, and leaves from trees in an attempt to keep alive. Without proper nutrition they easily fell sick and by 1847 typhus and cholera were raging amongst the famine victims. Little more than skeletons in rags, many shut themselves in their huts and waited to die.

It is not known precisely how many people died during the Great Famine; historians estimate that it may have been as many as one million. Another two million people emigrated during the famine, most of them to America. All in all, during these years Ireland lost between a quarter and a third of her population to starvation, disease, and emigration.

During the famine, some landlords attempted to evict tenants who had not paid their rent. The artists of the painting above and the engraving below wanted to rouse public opinion in Britain against the evictions. The bottom picture shows a fat, well-dressed landlord forcing a starving, sick family out of their home. He has brought soldiers to back up his authority.

Fleeing the famine

Because of the emigration of earlier years, the emigrant's route to North America was well known, but whereas before it had often been the more prosperous people who had emigrated, now the poorest of the poor began to leave. The motivation for emigration had changed, too. Once people went optimistically to North America in search of a better life; now they simply wanted to escape Ireland. As one group of famine victims said: *"All we want is to get out of Ireland. We must be better anywhere than here."*

Some landlords paid for their former tenants to emigrate; although costly, this allowed the landlords to clear small, inefficient tenant farms off their estates. Many others financed the voyage with money sent back home to Ireland from relatives who had already emigrated. During the famine, Irish people abroad sent back many thousands of dollars a year to help their relatives leave Ireland.

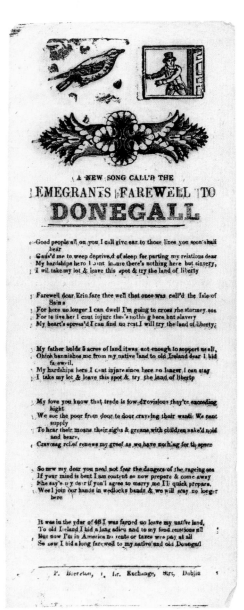

A NEW SONG CALL'D THE
EMEGRANTS FAREWEEL TO
DONEGALL

No safe passage

The journey for most people fleeing the famine was wretched. Initially, the emigrants had to get to England, as most of the ships for North America sailed from Liverpool. The most destitute crossed the Irish Sea in open-topped cattle boats and coal barges. Once in Britain thousands were too poor to travel any further and settled instead in working-class slums in Liverpool, London, and Glasgow. Many died of fever and those lucky enough to survive were shunned by the locals, who accused them of bringing disease and poverty to their neighborhoods.

For those who could afford to go on to North America, a perilous voyage lay ahead. Many of the emigrants were robbed by tricksters even before they left Liverpool. Others spent all their savings on expensive lodgings and by the time they left were virtually penniless. The ships were usually overcrowded and cramped and the food and water supplies were often inadequate for the four- to six-week voyage. Not all the ships arrived; between 1847 and 1853, some 57 ships bound for North America were lost at sea.

Floating coffins

Disease was so bad on the ships that they became known as floating coffins. Over half of the passengers died on some ships. Frightened that the disease would spread to their own populations, American and Canadian authorities often held up the ships at quarantine stations until the disease had exhausted itself. In the summer of 1847 the

Many emigrants left Ireland reluctantly and this inspired some popular songs. This emigrant's song tells the story of a man's departure from Ireland because of poverty and of the wealth that he found in America.

quarantine authorities at Grosse Ile in Canada were overwhelmed by the arrival of more than forty ships all carrying diseased famine victims. Within weeks, thousands had died. A monument erected in their memory reads: *"In this secluded spot lie the mortal remains of 5424 persons who flying from Pestilence and Famine in Ireland in the year 1847 found in America but a Grave."*

Despite the dangers, most emigrants thought that they had no choice but to leave Ireland. Poverty and starvation awaited them if they stayed. But many Catholic emigrants believed that they had been driven out of their country by British misgovernment and English hostility to Catholics.

Many ships competed for passengers across the Atlantic. On board conditions below deck were cramped and dark, as the drawing above shows. Disease thrived in these "floating coffins."

Fire was another big hazard for the emigrants on wooden sailing ships. The *Ocean Monarch* (left) caught fire and sank in August 1848. Almost 180 emigrants, over half of those on board, died in the tragedy.

The Post-famine Exodus

"Lose no time to come to the goldfields there will be gold had here for ages to come let all friends and neighbors come as soon as possible."

In spite of Ireland's extraordinary loss of population during the famine years, emigration from Ireland continued at an even greater level after it. From 1851 until 1921, between 4 and 4.5 million people left Ireland. The overwhelming majority, more than 3 million, emigrated to the United States. Of the remainder, at least 500,000 went to Britain, 200,000 to Canada, and another 300,000 to Australia and New Zealand.

In the 1850s steamers began to replace the old sailing ships. The steamers were built to carry passengers and, most importantly, were much quicker than the old ships. By the mid 1860s most emigrants traveled to North America by steamer, on a voyage lasting about 12 to 14 days instead of the 4 to 6 weeks it used to take. Much of the fear and danger of the long voyage across the Atlantic had disappeared.

Most of the emigrants who left Ireland in these years were Catholic peasants and laborers from the poorest provinces of Ireland, Connaught, and Munster. The biggest cause of emigration continued to be the poor opportunities that people had for work and prosperity in Ireland.

Before the famine, farmers used to divide up their land among their sons, so that each adult male had at least a tiny patch of land to work for himself. The bitter experience of the famine, however, made Irish farmers more cautious. Many stopped sharing their land among their sons and instead gave it all to the eldest son. It was more efficient for one man to farm a larger patch of land, but it meant that all the other sons had to leave home in search of work. As farmers' sons could not find work, so farmers' daughters could not find husbands. Young unmarried men and women dominated the emigrant population after the famine – for decades Ireland lost her youngest and most productive adults to countries abroad.

Emigrants queue at the money exchange at Ellis Island, New York. This was the immigration office that controlled and recorded new arrivals to the United States.

Paying for the voyage

After the famine, emigrants continued to send money back to Ireland to pay for their relations to join them in their new country. Some of this came in the form of checks and money orders, but often emigrants bought tickets and mailed them to their relatives in Ireland with instructions as to which ship to catch and what to bring with them.

Government assistance also made it easier for some of the poorest people to emigrate. The government and the Irish Poor Law Boards financed the emigration of almost 80,000 destitute people to North America and another 100,000 people received assistance from the government to emigrate to Australia. Normally, it was too expensive for most people to travel to Australia. If people could prove, however, that they had some money and that they were good workers, the government would agree to pay for all or part of their journey to Australia. These were called assisted-passage schemes and they were set up to encourage land settlement in Australia.

Emigrants, even poor ones, dressed as respectably as they could on arrival in a new country, as the photograph above shows. Nevertheless, images of the Irish as incurably scruffy and untidy, like this one, persisted in magazines in Britain and America.

Thousands of Irish laborers helped build America's network of railroads. Many had emigrated to California in the 1850s and 1860s hoping to strike it rich in the goldfields.

Gold!

From the 1850s, the discovery of gold in North America, South Africa, Australia, and New Zealand spurred waves of young Irishmen to emigrate. Excited letters back to Ireland, such as that written in 1852 by an Irish policeman in Australia, instructed people to *"lose no time to come to the goldfields there will be gold had here for ages to come let all friends and neighbors come as soon as possible."*

In America, the discovery of gold in California encouraged many Irish who had already settled on the east coast to make the long trek to the west.

A few prospectors got lucky, but most soon realized that there was more money to be made in running businesses to service the townships springing up around the goldfields. In the wake of the gold rush, thousands of Irish laborers were hired by railroad companies to build tracks crisscrossing the American plains. The railroad camps were often like Irish villages on the move, with Irish diggers, tracklayers, carpenters, blacksmiths, and clerks. To people in Ireland, America seemed never to have enough laborers.

Gold-digging was hard and uncertain work. Many found that there was more regular money to be made working on the railroads.

Irish Women in America

Most Irish women emigrants chose their husbands from among the large number of Irish men already settled in America.

After the famine, large numbers of women began to leave Ireland. From 1881 to 1910 almost 800,000 women emigrated, actually outnumbering the male emigrants in these years. Most of them traveled alone. They were usually young, aged about 21, and unmarried. Some took government-assisted passages to Australia, but most, over 80 percent of them, went to America.

Women left Ireland because they lacked opportunities for employment and financial independence. Traditionally they had earned money by spinning linen and wool at home, but now they were unable to compete with the cheap yarn made by factories in Britain. Without an income, it was difficult to marry, and increasingly Irish girls discovered that they were expected to stay at home, living as cheaply as possible. Faced with such a bleak future, thousands of spirited young women took the leap across the Atlantic in search of work and a partner.

▲ Cheap yarns produced in British factories destroyed the traditional livelihood of many Irish women, who used to spin yarn in their cottages.

It was mainly young unmarried women who took the brave step of crossing the Atlantic to America. They had little hope of work or marriage in Ireland. ▶

Working lives

Like the post-famine emigration of young men, most of the women emigrants were from the two poorest provinces of Ireland, Connaught, and Munster, and most were Catholics. Nearly all of them settled in American cities and took jobs as domestic servants, factory millhands, or needleworkers. Work in textile mills was dangerous and underpaid; most of the women preferred domestic service if they could get it. Needlework was also badly paid but for many Irish women it was still an improvement on their

Irish women in America often took jobs as waitresses like these in Childs, New York, in 1900. Local American girls thought that working as a waitress or a servant was beneath them, but for the Irish women these jobs gave them a respectable income.

The dreams of wealth in America did not always come true. In the 1860s, some Irish women immigrants lived in a makeshift village they built for themselves in Central Park, New York.

situation in Ireland. One woman who found work as a seamstress in Connecticut, wrote happily to her sister in Ireland, saying: *"I am getting along splendid and likes my work . . . it seems like a new life. I will soon have a trade and be more independent . . . you know it was always what I wanted so I have reached my highest ambition."*

Saving for the future

Many Irish women found work as domestic servants. Prejudice against Irish serving girls was strong; their American mistresses often said that they were slovenly and stupid. Whatever the insults, domestic service paid better wages than factory work. From it, Irish women learned and copied middle-class behavior. Accommodation, food, and sometimes even a uniform came with the job, allowing a servant to save nearly all of her wages. Irish women sent back money to their families in Ireland and gave generously to the Catholic Church, which helped fund Catholic schools and hospitals in America.

Most Irish women emigrants married Irish men already settled in America. As mothers, many made sure that their American-born daughters did not have to work as servants or in factories. They educated their daughters for white-collar jobs and took pride in seeing them gain positions as teachers, nurses, secretaries, and salesgirls.

The Irish Outside Ireland

Irish people's experience of emigration varied from country to country and different Irish communities developed in America, Britain, Canada, and Australia. One thing, however, was the same in all four countries: they were all English-speaking, Protestant countries. Catholics were in a minority and were often distrusted by the Protestants who suspected that the Catholics' loyalty to the pope came before loyalty to their new country. In addition, the Protestant Irish emigrants were wealthier and better skilled than most of the Catholic emigrants. They did not get trapped in laboring jobs in city slums and so did not stand out as a separate group in the way that Irish Catholic laborers did. What often appeared to be prejudice against the Irish was actually prejudice against the Irish Catholics.

Rural lives in Canada and Australia

Most of the Irish who migrated to Canada and Australia found work in rural communities, in fishing, timber, and farming. Most of Canada's Irish were not poverty-stricken and over half of them were Protestants, mostly skilled farmers from Ulster. In Australia too, apart from the convicts, the Irish immigrants were seldom penniless. Protestant settlers complained about the arrival of Irish Catholic immigrants in both countries, but such opposition does not appear to have held the Irish Catholics back. Within a few years of arriving in Canada and Australia, many immigrants, Catholic and Protestant alike, were able to buy their own farms or establish trading stores and hotels.

From 8.5 million in 1845, the beginning of the famine, the population plummeted to 4.3 million in 1926.

The Irish who settled in Australia often became farmers. Their homes would have been similar to the farm on this page in New South Wales.

A Catholic priest blesses a group of emigrants. Irish Catholics often paid for Irish priests and nuns to join them in their new countries.

Popular images of the Irish as stupid and lazy laborers persisted for many years, long after they had begun to achieve success in middle-class professions. This cartoon shows a common prejudice about the Irish as drinkers and beggars.

▼ One route to respectability for Irish immigrants in Britain and the United States was the army. These are men from the Irish Guards in the British army. The U.S. army also had several all-Irish units.

Urban workers in America and Britain

A different picture developed in America and Britain, especially after the famine. There few Irish became farmers. America and Britain got the poorest of Ireland's emigrants. Unskilled and often destitute on arrival, they took jobs for less money than local workers would accept; as a result, the locals blamed them for lowering wages and worsening working conditions. The Irish were also accused of spreading disease, violence, and drunkenness.

Anti-Irish prejudice grew, taking various forms. Magazine cartoons showed the Irish as stupid, monkey-like laborers and newspapers carried advertisements for servants, cooks, and clerks that included the statement: "No Irish need apply." In some cases the hostility erupted into violence. Britain's first recorded riot against the Irish occurred in Manchester in 1807. In Philadelphia in 1844, supporters of the Native American Party, which opposed the immigration of Irish Catholics to America, rampaged through the city's Irish neighborhoods, killing 30 people and destroying three Catholic churches and 200 homes.

Prosperity and independence

In spite of their lowly start, poor Irish Catholic immigrants, especially in America, greatly improved their income and social status. By the late 19th century nearly every fireman and policeman in New York, Boston, and Chicago was an Irishman. So strong was their hold over these professions that the Irish were able to prevent locals and other immigrants from gaining jobs in them. The Irish also often took the lead in trade unions and many went on to influential political careers in the Democratic Party of America. In San Francisco, the Irish became well-known as businessmen involved in transportation, mining, and real estate.

In all of their new countries, Catholic Irish immigrants gave generously to the Catholic Church, but nowhere was the effect quite so dramatic as in America where the Irish transformed Catholicism from a minority religion into a wealthy and politically influential organization that boasted a nationwide network of churches, schools, colleges, and hospitals. The church became a powerful symbol of Irish identity and self-help in America, and the education provided by its schools enabled many American-born children of Irish immigrants to enter middle-class professions like law, medicine, and teaching.

Lasting resentment against the British

Even though Irish Catholics abroad often achieved a degree of prosperity that they could never have had as laborers and poor farmers in Ireland, they still thought of themselves as victims of Ireland's tragic history of poverty, famine, and British misrule. As a result, Irish Catholic immigrants and their descendants were strong supporters of the Irish struggle for independence from British rule.

In the late 19th and early 20th centuries, Irish Catholics in America, Britain, and Australia helped fund the Home Rule movement and the war of independence that culminated in the creation of the Irish Free State in 1921. Irish Americans have often given money and political support to Sinn Fein and the Irish Republican Army (IRA) for their campaign to end British rule in Northern Ireland.

▲ The building of the grand St. Patrick's Cathedral in New York was for many Irish Catholics a symbol that they had become an important and respected part of American society.

▼ In the late 19th century, many police forces in the United States became dominated by Irish immigrants. A strong tradition of Irish-American policemen continues today.

The Mohawk members of this Orange Lodge in Ontario, Canada, are far removed from the politics of Orange Lodges in Northern Ireland.

After the famine, empty villages and rural decay became a common sight in Ireland. For decades Ireland's young people went abroad in search of work and prosperity.

Orange Lodges

Perhaps because Protestants were better able to fit in to their new countries, they did not feel such a strong need to retain a separate identity as Irishmen. In Canada the Irish Protestants established many Orange Lodges, exclusively Protestant societies that swore to protect the 1801 Act of Union between Britain and Ireland. In Ireland today these societies are still overtly political organizations, dedicated to preserving British rule in Northern Ireland, but in Canada they have become more like social and charitable clubs. In Newfoundland, for example, the local Orange order runs a hospital open to people of all religious denominations, not just Protestants.

A depleted land

During the 19th century, Ireland lost a vast number of people, mostly through emigration. From 8.5 million in 1845, the beginning of the famine, the population plummeted to 4.3 million in 1926. Without emigration, the history of Ireland would have been different. Emigration acted as a safety valve, channeling waves of poor and frustrated people to other countries. Had these people stayed, Ireland would have experienced more popular unrest and possibly even a socialist revolution.

There were other consequences as well. The huge sums of money sent back by emigrants in America helped to preserve in Ireland an old-fashioned way of life. As her European neighbors entered the 20th century, Ireland,

Irish people around the world celebrate St. Patrick's Day on March 17 to help keep alive their sense of belonging to Ireland. St. Patrick is the patron or father saint of Ireland.

he St. Patrick Day's greeting card above uses everal symbols of Irish culture to create ostalgia for Ireland: the Irish harp, the hamrock (clover-leaf) of St. Patrick, and the ipe. Erin is a traditional name for Ireland.

deprived of her most adventurous citizens and artificially supported by the American remittances, carried on with a culture and economy that seemed frozen in time. Ireland did not modernize or industrialize; into the 20th century her principal export continued to be cheap labor.

In 1921, the Irish Free State came into being. For years nationalists had been predicting that, once Ireland was freed from British rule, emigration would cease. This did not happen. Ireland's economy had been too severely damaged by the long and unequal relationship with Britain's more powerful industrial economy. Young Irish men and women continued to emigrate, mainly to Britain but also to America and Australia. The population in the Irish Free State continued to fall until the 1960s, when increased overseas investment created better employment prospects. In Northern Ireland, which is still under British rule, emigration has increased in the last 30 years, as violence between Catholics and Protestants has blighted people's lives and driven away industry and tourism.

A global Irish community

The emigration of the Irish over the last two centuries built up distinctive Irish communities all around the English-speaking world. The emigrants re-created bits of Irish culture in their new countries, often centering on the Catholic Church, St. Patrick's Day celebrations, or if they were Protestant, Orange Lodges. Irish social clubs and bars or hotels are common in many parts of Britain, America, Canada, and Australia.

The Irish who have emigrated in this century have been able to keep up their ties with relations in Ireland more easily than the people who emigrated in the 18th and 19th centuries. Today, however, many descendants of these early emigrants travel to Ireland to try to trace their ancestors and their family's Irish origins.

Timeline

1610 Protestants from England and Scotland begin to settle in Ulster, northern Ireland.

1641 Catholic rebellion against Protestants in Ulster: Catholics in Ireland support the Royalists against Oliver Cromwell and the Puritans in the Civil War; on crushing the rebellion, the Puritans confiscate the land of the Irish rebels and give it to English Protestants.

1690 Battle of the Boyne, Ulster: William of Orange, the new Protestant King of England, defeats James II, the old Catholic King of England, who has been fighting the English in Ireland with Irish and French Catholic support; William's victory cements the British control of Ireland.

1695 "Penal Laws": Catholics are forbidden from possessing weapons and good horses; their rights to education are limited; more anti-Catholic laws follow over the next 50 years.

1728 Catholics are denied the vote.

1760s-70s Ulster migration to colonial North America: thousands of people from the northern province of Ulster, often people of Scottish descent, leave Ireland for North America.

1792 Catholic Relief Act: Catholics are allowed to work as lawyers; over the next 40 years Britain gradually abolishes the laws against Catholics.

1798 Bloody rebellion against British rule in Ireland.

1801 Act of Union between Britain and Ireland: Irish parliament in Dublin is abolished and Ireland is now ruled direct from the British parliament at Westminster in London.

1829 Catholic Emancipation Act: Catholics can be elected to the British Parliament and be employed in the government and the army.

1845-49 The Great Famine.

1870 Beginning of the Home Rule movement: a movement in Ireland, supported by some British politicians, to give Ireland a parliament to make laws on local issues like education, taxation, agriculture, and manufacturing.

1879-82 Irish Land War: Irish tenant farmers rise up in protest against their landlords and demand fair rents and secure leases of land.

1881 The Land Act: Gladstone, the British Prime Minister, grants the Irish farmers' demands; landlord power in Ireland begins to weaken.

1914-18 World War I: The British Parliament suspends plans for Irish Home Rule for the duration of the war.

1916 Easter Rising: About 1200 Irish nationalists seize government buildings in central Dublin and proclaim Irish independence; they are quickly captured and their leaders are executed by the British.

1921 Creation of the Irish Free State: after vicious fighting between Irish nationalists and British troops, the British grant independence to southern Ireland and the Irish Free State or Éire is created; most of the northern province of Ulster stays in the union with Britain.

1939-45 World War II: Ireland remains neutral during the war and does not support Britain or her allies in the war against Hitler's Germany.

1948 Republic of Ireland Act: The Irish Free State becomes the Republic of Ireland and leaves the British Commonwealth.

1958 Industrial Development Act, Ireland: Ireland invites overseas countries to build factories in Ireland so as to create employment and prevent its young people from emigrating.

1968-95 "The Troubles," Northern Ireland: Catholics in Northern Ireland protest against Protestant discrimination against Catholics; the Irish Republican Army (IRA) begins a campaign of bombing and terrorism in Northern Ireland and Britain designed to end the British control of Northern Ireland and to reunite the north with the south; violence increases between Catholics and Protestants.

1969 British Army sent to Northern Ireland: British soldiers attempt to keep the peace between Catholics and Protestants, but violence continue

1994 IRA ceasefire: IRA agrees to suspend fighting; talks planned to settle peacefully the crisis in Northern Ireland.

1996 IRA ceasefire ends but peace efforts continue.

Glossary

Aborigines: the original inhabitants of Australia.

Act of Union: the law that came into force on January 1, 1801, abolishing Ireland's independent parliament in Dublin and uniting Ireland in a single political body with England, Scotland, and Wales, ruled by the British Houses of Parliament at Westminster in London.

arable land: land which is fit for growing cereal crops, such as wheat and barley.

bureaucracy: a system of government in which the government workers have fixed jobs and follow fixed rules; the system by which government regulations are administered.

Catholic/Roman Catholic: a Christian who recognizes the pope as God's representative on earth and accepts his teachings and interpretations of the Bible as God's truth.

chain gang: a gang of prisoners or convicts who are chained together to prevent them from escaping while working outdoors.

cholera: a human disease carried by dirty water that causes diarrhea and severe dehydration.

emigrate: to leave one's country to settle permanently in another country.

evict: to force someone out of their home or off their land.

Gaelic: the original Celtic language of Ireland; also of Scotland.

Home Rule: a campaign in Ireland and Britain in the late 19th century to allow the Irish to make their own laws concerning local issues, such as education and taxation, while allowing Britain to keep control of matters like foreign affairs and defense.

immigrate: to arrive in a new country, intending to stay permanently.

Industrial Revolution: the period of rapid economic change in the late 18th and early 19th century Britain, marked by the growth of factories and machinery to manufacture products cheaply and in large numbers.

Irish Republican Army (IRA): Irish military group, founded in about 1919, to fight for Irish independence; since the 1960s in particular it has carried on a terrorist campaign in both Britain and Northern Ireland designed to defeat British rule in Northern Ireland.

penal colony: a country or island, often in an isolated part of the world, which is used by another country as a jail; prisoners who are sent there have no way of leaving the colony or getting back to their own country; "penal" is an adjective relating to punishment, penalties, or prison.

prejudice: an opinion against someone or something that has been made without knowing anything about that person or subject; someone who says "I don't like Irish people" but who has never met any Irish people is prejudiced.

prospectors: people who look for minerals in the ground such as gold, diamonds, silver, and copper.

Protestant: a Christian who does not believe that the pope is God's leader on earth and who rejects some of the practices and beliefs of the Roman Catholic church; the first Protestants separated from the Roman Catholic church in the 16th century in a movement known as the Reformation.

quarantine: a system of keeping people with infectious diseases in isolation so that the disease cannot spread to healthy people.

real estate: property in buildings and land.

St. Patrick's Day: an annual celebration on March 17 of parades, dances, and church services, commemorating St. Patrick's introduction of Christianity to Ireland in the 5th century.

Sinn Fein: Irish political party, meaning "Ourselves Alone," founded in 1905 to campaign for Irish independence; since the creation of the Irish Free State in 1921, Sinn Fein has campaigned for the British to leave Northern Ireland and for the north and south to be reunited under one independent Irish government. Sinn Fein are closely associated with the IRA.

socialist revolution: an uprising by the workers of a country to overthrow the rich people and create a government in which money, property, and education are distributed equally among all of the people.

tenant farmers: farmers who do not own farming land but rent it instead from a landlord.

typhus: a human disease spread by lice and causing fever, headaches, and rashes.

Index